D0519562

MARY WILSON

SELECTED POEMS

Mary Wilson

SELECTED
POEMS

ARROW BOOKS

Arrow Books Ltd
3 Fitzroy Square, London W1

An imprint of the Hutchinson Publishing Group

London Melbourne Sydney Auckland
Wellington Johannesburg and agencies
throughout the world

First published by
Hutchinson & Co (Publishers) Ltd 1970
Arrow edition 1973
This edition 1976
© Mary Wilson 1970

Made and printed in Great Britain
by The Anchor Press Ltd
Tiptree, Essex

ISBN 0 09 907980 1

To my husband

CONTENTS

———◆———

[7]

SCILLONIAN POEMS

——◆——

RECENT POEMS

——◆——

[9]

PREFACE

P EOPLE often ask me why I write poetry. I suppose one reason may be that when I was a small child I was taken to church every Sunday, and consequently came to know the splendid imagery of the Bible, and also of course, became familiar with the hymns which were sung, many of which were written by well-known poets, so that it seemed quite natural to me to want to express my thoughts in verse; and, so far as I remember, I wrote my first poem when I was about six years old.

I am happiest writing poetry which rhymes and scans, although I have written a little free verse. Rhyming poetry is fairly difficult to write; if you submit to the discipline of rhyme and metre, it is important to try to steer a course between doggerel and over-flowery metaphor, full of adjectives inserted to correct the metre, and sometimes the particular word you want to use is difficult to fit into the framework.

Reading poetry brings me great happiness. If I have a preference, it is for writers of country poetry, with descriptions of country scenes—Keats, Tennyson, Emily Brontë, Thomas Hardy; but I enjoy reading all poetry, although perhaps the austerities of Pope and Milton and the obscurities of Browning need a little more thought!

I think the charm of poetry lies in the fact that it can

capture an emotion, or describe a scene or happening without any preliminaries or stage-setting, and that it is possible to find a poem to match every mood.

Mary Wilson.

EARLY
POEMS

———◆———

Iғ I can write, before I die
One line of purest poetry;
Or crystallize, for all to share
A thought unique, a moment rare
Within one sentence, clear and plain—
Then I shall not have lived in vain.

The Virgin's Song

O the wild gladness of the waiting spirit
Which hears, like music on a distant horn
The first sweet, silver notes of coming rapture—
The music of a love as yet unborn.

Which trembles at a touch, whoe'er the giver,
Or springs, at sight of love, into full flower,
Or prays in purity, with fingers folded
For consummation of its waited hour.

Which, rising when the East with light is flooded,
Stands silent with expectant arms outflung
To greet the sun unrisen, the rose unbudded,
The book unopened, and the song unsung.

False, foolish hopes of ecstasy eternal!
The enraptured moment comes, is grasped, is gone!
Yet through the lengthening years we seek it ever,
And youth's remembered longing drives us on.

The Hedonist

If I must die, as die I must
First let me fully live,
And grasp and hold a thousand joys,
And take as well as give.

And let me no experience miss,
But taste and savour all,
And dance throughout the dazzling day
On which the dark will fall.

And may the pattern of my life
Lie strand on scarlet strand
'Til God leans from His sapphire throne—
The hour-glass in His hand.

Winter Parting

Do you remember walking in the Park
In the red sunset of a winter's day?
The grass was frosty, and the lake was dark;
You told me that you had to go away.

'Mary,' you said, and 'Mary!' once again;
You grasped my cold, cold hands within your own
Too tightly, but I did not feel the pain,
I could not think or speak—my heart was stone.

How cold it was, my love, how cold, how cold
In the long twilight when the sun had fled!
The day was dying, and the year was old.
'Why have we wasted so much time?' you said.

And now the summer trees are full of leaf;
The lake reflects the shining blue above;
But still I cannot put away my grief,
Nor have I learned to live without your love.

Outside, the snow is falling; all the land
Is silent, and a soft serenity
Rests on our hearts, as we lie hand in hand
In that deep peace which follows ecstasy.

And this we know—even while foolish tears
Spring to our eyes as we go on alone—
We have known beauty which will last the years,
And love which men have died for, and not known.

And so, my darling, free from bitterness,
We gaze upon that Eden we must leave,
And, sighing, turn to face the Wilderness—
Regretful Adam, and reluctant Eve.

O that we might, for one brief hour
Forget that we are bound apart,
And lie within each other's arms
Mouth pressed on mouth, and heart on heart.

For just one hour from all our life
To sink unchained through passion's deep
And, cast upon the farther shore
To lie entwined in tender sleep!

The Train

How like a man to choose a crowded train
To say that we must never meet again!
Or was it masculine low cunning
So that I could not make a scene?
It might have been.

O anguish as the suburbs clattered by!
We had to shout to make our voices heard,
But still I understood each telling word—
'We can't go on like this,
I thought you understood;
You must see it's no good.'

Like statues we were standing in the corridor
And people, pushing past with cases
Glared at us both for being in the way,
And I said all the bitter things
I had not meant to say.

I put dark glasses on to hide my eyes,
But then I could not see your face
To see if I had hurt you
But I hoped I had.
Oh, I behaved with little grace.

And still you stood there, silent and unbending.
God! What an ending!

To Robin, when a Baby

SOUNDLY he sleeps, heavy upon the pillow,
Knees bent in comfort, fingers tightly curled,
Gently quiescent, helpless, unprotected,
Trusting in slumber to a clement world.

Strange that this child, once linked with me so closely,
Born of my body, nourished at my breast—
Is now a separate entity, a Being,
Remote, apart from me, his thoughts unguessed.

And that within this little quiet body
Unknown and sleeping, lie his future years;
His dreams, his hopes, his longings and ambitions,
His loves, his hates, his heartaches and his fears.

Soundly he sleeps, heavy upon the pillow,
Knees bent in comfort, fingers tightly curled,
Gently quiescent, helpless, unprotected,
Man of the future—heir to all the world!

The house at the edge of the wood

SOMETIMES, as I struggle through crowded rooms
Thick with tobacco and whisky fumes,
And vapid voices shrilling high
In one continuous parrot cry—

Suddenly, I can see it there!
I can see the bluebells, can smell the air,
And the evening sunlight slants in lines
Across my house at the edge of the pines.

And a heavenly, healing silence falls
Upon my soul, and the caging walls
Melt, and the clanging voices die,
And we are alone, my house and I.

Somehow, someday, I shall be free
To go to the place where it waits for me;
For ever and ever my house has stood,
And all its windows face the wood.

SCILLONIAN
POEMS

The Isles of Scilly

NATURE is not more gentle here
Than in the city's crowded core;
For suddenly dark clouds appear,
Great waves beat up along the shore,

And on their crests black seaweed floats
Adrift in rain and driving spray
While all the gaily coloured boats
Rock at their moorings in the bay.

But when at last the storm is spent
The sun bursts out with burning force,
And draws towards the sky the scent
Of rain-washed earth, and rocks and gorse.

And, thrusting through the thinning haze,
Each little island gleams anew,
Its long white beaches all ablaze
With shining shells of every hue.

Now, when the starry dusk comes down,
With what a sure tranquillity
The lights glow from the little town!
And lights flash back across the sea

From watchers round the coast, who keep
Night-long their vigil without rest,
That all of us may safely sleep
Among the Islands of the Blest.

St. Agnes

Could I but live here all alone!
Alone with rocks and sea and sky,
Hearing no footsteps but my own,
And scream of wind, and curlew's cry,

And when the storm sweeps through the bay,
Standing amidst its angry roar
Deep, deep to breathe the salty spray
Flung up along the streaming shore!

So, when at last I come to die
May it be in these Isles I love—
On some rough seaward slope to lie,
The rocky turf piled high above;

Part of this pagan earth to be,
Part of the gorse's golden fire—
This will be immortality
And all the heaven I shall desire.

St. Mary's Church

THE fog is lifting, and the warning gun
At last is silent from the Bishop Rock;
Round Island lighthouse stops its weary moan,
And on this afternoon of early spring
Here in the church, the shaken candles weep.
Time passes, and the struggling daylight falls
From the great Schiller window; and the scent
Of hymnbooks, daffodils and holiness
Blends in a tranquillizing harmony.
Deep joy and searing grief are one, as if
A calming hand were laid upon the heart.

Tresco

Wʜᴇɴ the laughter and the shouting
Have faded at last from the quay,
Evening stillness comes to Tresco
And the wind blows in from the sea.

And the cows pad home for milking
Along the sandy bay
Through the tangy stalks of fennel
And the mounds of gathered hay.

Let us walk to Cromwell's Castle
Far over the scented Down.
Where the heather spreads its purple
And the bracken is turning brown.

And we'll count the lighthouse flashes
Across the darkening sky
Where the first pale stars are shining
As the fishing boats go by.

The Treasure

Silver piled high on silver, gold on gold,
Doubloons and guineas, crowns, pieces of eight—
Proof of a legend, and a tale re-told—
Cannons and rings, and piles of precious plate;
Here lies the treasure in a glittering heap,
Splendid and shining, dredged up from the deep.

On this bright autumn morning, all is still;
The sun burns down upon the quiet quay,
The flag is hardly stirring on the hill,
The boats glide in across a milky sea.
Only a fishing shag disturbs the peace,
Splashing and plunging where the breakers cease.

But on that eve of storm so long ago
O what a crashing tumult tore the sky!
The thundering clouds above, the rocks below,
The shrieks of drowning men, the sea-gulls' cry—
Down sank the ships, their pride and glory fled,
Their treasure spilling to the dark sea-bed.

Five stately frigates of the British line—
The flag-ship with the Admiral aboard;
He stood erect, in lawn and velvet fine,
Stern on the bridge, bejewelled hand on sword;
But he was cast up on Porthellick Bay
And robbed of all his riches where he lay.

Fast on the craggy Gilstone lay the fleet—
Until a diver, treading through the gloom
Felt the thick crunch of gold beneath his feet,
And stood a-dazzle in the rocky room
And saw, as if cast by some giant hand
A golden carpet all across the sand!

So here the treasure glows as if alive:
And yet across the triumph falls a thought—
That 'though these discs of metal still survive
In all their beauty, delicately wrought,
While they were lying underneath the tide
Hundreds of islanders have lived and died.

O how they loved to see the tall ships pass!
When in the long and burning summer days
They would row out across a sea of glass
Far to the westward, where the sun's last rays
Set all the heavens and the sea on fire
Beyond the Western Rocks and Castle Bryher.

And in the winter, when the islands rode
Like ships upon the anger of the sea,
Each man would fortify his small abode
Against the eager gale's ferocity,
And in his house of stone, secure and warm
King in his castle, would defy the storm.

In fishing, making kelp, and building boats
The islanders would pass each busy day,
Pausing to watch the seaweed where it floats,
Or see the children, tiring of their play
Run shouting home to fire and candle-gleam
Before the darkness, and the lighthouse beam.

Bright gorse and heather open to the light,
Gay shells tide-strewn along the windy shore,
Slow wash of waves in the sweet summer night—
All these they knew, and loved, and know no more.
They lived their island lives, and they are gone;
Yes, they are dust for whom the sun once shone.

The Lifeboat

We hear the rocket from the slip,
Fast, fast we run to watch them go,
Here in the dark we only know
That Scilly Rock has claimed a ship.

We see them as we cross the strand—
The smiling boatmen from the quay
Stern oil-skinned strangers seem to be,
Passing the ropes from hand to hand.

Old Matt looks on with wistful face;
He's had his share of risks and fears—
Coxswain or crew for sixty years—
And now young Matt stands in his place.

Now Doctor Bell climbs in the boat,
The pulleys turn, the cables lift
Into the water, smooth and swift
One rush of spray, and she's afloat.

Thank God there is no fog tonight
But tearing gale and streaming rain,
No stars to guide her home again,
Only the steady harbour light.

The evil rock waits in the gloom
Crouched like a beast beneath the waves,
Careless of all the lives she saves,
Eager to trick her to her doom.

A bobbing cork beside the wreck,
They cast a line to pull her in,
Half-deafened by the tempest's din
Which roars above the slippery deck.

And we can only stand and pray,
And as the chilly hours creep by
Watch for the paling of the sky;
How long it seems to wait for day!

Is that her engine? Yes, at last,
'All's well, all safe!' we hear them shout,
She edges in, and comes about,
Her journey done, her danger past.

RECENT
POEMS

After the Bomb

AFTER the Bomb had fallen,
After the last sad cry
When the Earth was a burn-out cinder
Drifting across the sky,

Came Lucifer, Son of the Morning,
With his fallen-angel band,
Silent and swift as a vulture
On a mountain-top to stand.

And he looked, as he stood on the mountain
With his scarlet wings unfurled,
At the charnel-house of London
And the cities of the world.

And he laughed. . . . .

And as that mocking laughter
Across the heavens ran,
He cried 'Look!' to the fallen angels—
'This is the work of *Man*
Who was made in the image of God!'

On Returning Home

T HE flowers are so gay, and the grass is so green,
The gardens have hedges, the pavements are clean,
The policemen are tall, and the people are neat
And sometimes they smile as they walk in the street.

They're cleaning Lord Nelson against the grey sky
—He stares with *both* eyes as the 'buses grind by;
The blackbird and thrush are beginning to sing,
And in London, in England, it soon will be Spring!

He lives on the steps of Central Hall
And buys his food from the coffee stall;
A tattered bundle protects his head
From the gritty pavement of his bed.

Every morning you'll see him there—
Dirty and smelly, with matted hair;
His feet are bandaged, his clothes are rags,
All his possessions in paper bags.

'Lay-about, drop-out!' you glibly say,
And hastily look the other way;
But the gates of Hell stand open wide
For those who pass on the other side!

How true it is that London never sleeps!
The traffic's hum might be a lullaby
But for the homing aeroplane, which sweeps
Whining and thundering across the sky.

Each quarter-hour the faithful clocks chime out
With Big Ben flatly bringing up the rear;
And ships hoot on the river, revellers shout,
And even through my dreaming, I can hear

Back-firing cars, and an illegal horn;
And here in Central London, dogs still bark,
While all night long, like heralds of the dawn
The Chinese geese are honking in the Park!

WE came through the gloomy door
From the cloisters wet with snow
To the Abbey, lit high with candles,
And the Baby asleep below.

A moment of sudden joy
On a dreary winter's day—
Will you remember, I wonder
When the snow has melted away?

This Christmas Night

How sweet and clear above the sounds of war
The clamorous bells are pealing their delight!
The angels sing of glory, as they soar
Among the man-made stars, this Christmas night.

And, once again, with spices and with gold
Three Kings are riding through the sparkling snow
To this poor lodging in the bitter cold
Where Mary kneels within the lantern-glow

To watch her Baby lying in the hay,
And think about the wonder of His birth;
And as He sleeps, to fold her hands and pray
For peace to come upon this troubled earth.

If I could end my life on such a day—
Here as I stand upon this windy hill!
In one great rush of swirling mist
And vapour, to be swept away.

But this would be too great felicity;
Some bright uncaring antiseptic ward
With kindly strangers' hands to close my eyes
Will see my journey to eternity—

To endless solitude, yet endless company;
To endless music, endless silence too;
Where I shall yield up my identity
And become part of Thee, Thou all of me.

You have turned your back on Eden
And shut the garden-gates,
And tramped away through the bracken
To where your future waits.
And the apple lies where you let it fall;
And the serpent laughs at you over the wall.

But perhaps, as you write by your window
On a day of tender spring,
You will stop your work for a moment
To hear a blackbird sing,
And will catch an echo, soft and clear
Of far-away music you cannot hear.

'Was there ever a quiet garden
Where the golden apples hung?
Where I walked with my love in the morning
Of the world, when we both were young,
And the serpent shone with an oily gleam?
Or was it only the dream of a dream?'

Winter Meeting

How shall I ever face them at the Meeting?
The train roars on through meadows piled with snow,
And constantly its rhythm keeps repeating
'He should have telephoned me hours ago'.

'There is a call for you!'—I hurry, hurry,
I hear him speaking, thin and far away,
'I had a breakdown, mother, did you worry?'
'Of course not, but I'm glad that you're O.K.'

Kind faces, smiling, turn to me in greeting;
The chairman raps the table, voices cease.
'I am so glad to be here at the Meeting!'
A mind that's tranquil, and a heart at peace.

Oxford

Young voices echo from the walls
Along the teeming High,
Peak upon peak St. Mary's soars
Against the summer sky.

And hesitating Merton clock
Chimes out each quarter-hour,
And strong and clear the time swings back
From nearby Magdalen tower.

How thick and green the Cherwell glides
Beneath a willow tree
Where in a punt a student lies,
His book upon his knee,

Struggling to cram his tired brain—
Finals loom over all;
Yet pausing every now and then
To hear the cuckoo call;

And in that cooing cry he hears
With pleasure and with pain,
The music of those three short years
He will not know again.

Millesgården, Stockholm

JEWELLED with statues, set-about with fountains—
A tangled garden, falling to the lake;
Granite and bronze and diabase and marble
A true memorial make

To one whose life was spent creating beauty,
Who made this garden slowly, year by year;
And now, from all the world they sail on Värtan
And find contentment here.

A pair of lovers rest beside the fountain
Eternally embracing, turned to stone,
Where, gazing at her own reflected image,
Susannah sits alone.

Down on the windy terrace by the water
Figures, earth-anchored, strain towards the sky—
Poseidon, from the sea, forever smiling;
Man on God's hand set high.

And over all, the water blowing, blowing,
Wetting the statues to a dripping gleam.
The flowers smell sweeter here in Millesgården
Within a sculptor's dream.

Aberfan

This is the valley where the stranger keeps his silence,
Where easy platitudes must not be spoken,
Where grief and bitter anger lay their burden
On those whose lives are broken.

Here, where we tread among the marble statues,
The flowers, and the fountain softly weeping,
Beneath the verses and the photographs
The little ones are sleeping.

Yet in the new school further down the valley
The children sing like blackbirds at the dawning;
No shades of memory lie on their faces
Lifted to greet the morning.

The stream runs on by the memorial garden,
The murd'rous tip of slag is disappearing;
Beyond the mountains, where the storm-clouds gathered
Slowly the sky is clearing.

Cambridgeshire

HUGE echoing churches guarded by flinty walls,
And long straight Roman roads where dusty sunlight
  falls,
And cream-brick houses patterned with flickering leaves
Where swallows build their clayey nests beneath the eaves;
And willows weeping where the river dallies by,
And, floating far above me, in the lark-hung sky
White clouds which throw their sailing shadows as they
  pass
On bloomy Cambridge meadows full of quaking-grass.

The Old Manse

O what a longing, and a burning deep desire
Here in my father's house, to be a child again;
To see the lamplight and the winter fire
Or smell the garden after summer rain!
    Just for a moment, Time is overset;
    The Past is now; the Present is not yet.

Syringa hangs its scent upon the early day
And white-heart cherries dangle from the clustering trees
Which, draped with threads to keep the birds away,
Shelter the rows of ripening strawberries.
    While in the cornfield by the garden-side
    Big poppies throw their crumpled petals wide.

Within the study, where the sunlight never falls
My father writes his sermon, hooded eyes down-bent;
His books of reference wait round the walls—
He shapes each phrase, deploys each argument
    And turns from time to time, instinctively
    To the great Bible, open on his knee.

I see my mother in the kitchen, making bread,
Setting the pliant dough in shallow pans to rise;
Her long brown hair is coiled around her head—
How young her form, how shining blue her eyes!
    The door stands open on the morning sweet,
    And all the hens come clucking to her feet.

My brother mounts his clean new bicycle to ride
The long white Cambridge road which winds up
    Windmill Hill,
I watch him disappear with shaky pride,
And then a silence wraps the garden, 'til
    My long-dead friend comes calling to the gate—
    The village school-bell clangs—we shall be late!

A start, and I awake—Time, with impatient hands
Has snatched away the picture from before my eyes;
Silent and empty now, the Old Manse stands,
Weedy and desolate, its garden lies.
    All, all is changed; and yet, it cannot be!
    Now is the dream—Then, the reality!

The Durham Miners' Gala

Suddenly we can hear the drums
Banging down the street;
And the brassy roaring of the bands,
And the rustle of marching feet,
And, with steadfast hands to hold them high
The silken banners go swaying by.

Bygone leaders and Bible scenes
Are woven on either side,
And the miners' lodge walks on before
Each banner, with solemn pride;
And the windows are full to see them go
And cheers rise up from the crowd below.

Police horses, stepping carefully
Clear a triumphant way
As the boys and girls come singing through
Dressed up for the holiday,
And they join their hands and dance, as they come,
To the silver music and thudding drum.

Then, all at once, the singing dies
For a banner draped in black;
And we can see the flickering lamps
Or hear the pit-props crack.
And the knowledge comes to each watching soul
That, now and ever, 'there's blood on the coal'.

Now on the platform the speakers wait,
Each one with uncovered head,
And the crowd below falls silent
As the Roll of Honour is read.
And when the final tributes are paid
We stand, as 'Gresford' is slowly played.

Those who have come to address the crowd
Make their voices heard,
And the people listen quietly
And carefully weigh each word.
The Meeting hears each speaker out—
But, here and there, a dissenting shout.

Balloons, released by little hands
Go rocking into the air,
And the sound of the hurdy-gurdy floats
From the roundabouts at the fair,
And we smell the river as we pass,
Onions, hamburgers, trampled grass.

Above the city's winding streets
The Cathedral stands alone,
And the sound of the bands is almost lost
In the lofty arches of stone.
The banners are blessed in the slanting sun—
And one more Gala Day is done.

WHEN in the night remorse returns to haunt me
And beat incessant drums inside my head,
And grief wells up for sympathy not given,
And lack of patient love for those now dead—

Then, in the darkness as I lie unsleeping,
Lost in the depths of three-o'clock despair,
The age-old cry comes to my mind unbidden
'Show me, O God, show me that you are there!'

But now a greyness creeps behind the curtain,
The birds awaken while it still is night
Blackbird and thrush, linnet and finch and starling,
Singing and carolling to greet the light.

High as the highest bell within the belfry,
In crystalline cascades of brilliant notes,
The chorus of the dawn, perfect in beauty
Rises in rapture from the beating throats.

And as the chilly air blows through the window,
The sun leaps upward in a yellow glow;
The last clear trembling voice falls into silence,
And am I answered now? I do not know.

I only know that as the daylight strengthens
The black dreams of the night are borne away;
I draw the curtain back to see the garden,
And hope is with me to begin the day.

The Lunarnaut

'What did the earth look like,' I asked him
'As you stood there on the moon?'

'Bright,' he said, 'Fantastically bright,
Brighter than any moonlit night—
A shining orb of dazzling light.

And we could see the countries clear as day
'Though miles of atmosphere between us lay,
And home and friends and loves were far away.'